Original title:
Life, the Universe, and Everything in Between

Copyright © 2025 Creative Arts Management OÜ
All rights reserved.

Author: Benjamin Caldwell
ISBN HARDBACK: 978-1-80566-000-2
ISBN PAPERBACK: 978-1-80566-295-2

## Uncharted Realms of Wonder

In space where socks go lost,
Planets spin with quirky cost.
Aliens dance in strange attire,
While we wish on stars that expire.

Comets made of jelly beans,
Orbiting in cosmic scenes.
Whispers float on solar winds,
Telling tales of space-time spins.

## A Tapestry of Dreams and Stars

Weaving tales with threads of light,
Shooting stars play hide and seek at night.
Clouds of candy, fluffy and sweet,
While moonbeams throw us a midnight treat.

In a universe with kitten paws,
Gravity giggles, defying laws.
Rainbows ride on galactic beams,
Chasing after our candy dreams.

## Fragments of Eternity

Time takes coffee breaks, it seems,
While we chase after silly dreams.
A toaster thinks it's time to fly,
As toast escapes to greet the sky.

Moments stretch like silly string,
Tick-tock clocks can hardly sing.
Each second trips on cosmic trails,
Winking at us with playful tales.

## The Rhythm of Unseen Forces

Dancing atoms keep the beat,
Chaotic rhythms, oh so sweet.
A quirk of fate with every glance,
While gravity leads the cosmic dance.

Bubbling laughter in a black hole,
Spinning galaxies lose control.
In this ballet of stars and quirks,
Even the void can't help but smirk.

## Celestial Journeys Unraveled

Stars wink and giggle bright,
Planets dance in cosmic flight.
Comets sneeze with tails so long,
Galaxies croon a silly song.

Black holes play hide and seek,
While meteors dramatically squeak.
Asteroids munch on spacey snacks,
Gravity shows its funny cracks.

# The Symphony of Being

Life's a tune, not too complex,
Bump the bass, oh what the heck!
Puppies howl and cats meow,
Join the band, don't ask how.

Join the rhythm, let's all sway,
Every moment's a cabaret.
Sing along with joy and glee,
Silly notes of harmony.

**Mosaic of Moments**

Pieces of the day collide,
With laughter as our trusty guide.
Jellybeans and shooting stars,
Play hopscotch on Venus' bars.

Time's a puzzle, not a race,
With giggles folded into space.
Every second shaped with cheer,
Let's make memories far and near.

**Enigmas Wrapped in Light**

What's the riddle of the night?
Twinkling bulbs brought forth with light.
Quasars giggle, black holes grin,
Who knew dark could wear such skin?

Cosmic puzzles with a flair,
Astro-antics in the air.
Laughter echoes, shadows tease,
Eureka! It's all just a breeze.

**Pulses of Distant Realities**

In a cafe of stars, I sip my tea,
Wondering if aliens drink it with glee.
Do they chatter in tongues, or just mime?
At light speed, who cares? It's all just a rhyme.

Floating through thoughts like balloons on a string,
In a universe spaced out, a merry old fling.
I tripped on a comet, and tumbled with grace,
Hope they don't charge me for this outer-space race.

## **Silhouettes on the Edge of Infinity**

Dancing in shadows, we spin and we twirl,
Chasing the sparkles that time likes to hurl.
With steps out of sync, we invent our own beat,
As the cosmos looks on, in bemused retreat.

Wormholes are just tunnels for having a laugh,
Riding the waves like a cosmic giraffe.
We're all just pirates, on ships made of air,
Sailing through nonsense, with stars in our hair.

## The Veils of Spacetime

Peeking behind curtains of light years and hues,
Catching a glimpse of the galaxy's hues.
A time traveler trips on a grass blade so green,
Asking, "Where's the pizza?" Like it's some kind of scene.

Through portals of laughter, we tumble and roll,
Finding the punchline that tickles the soul.
With giggles that echo in corners of night,
We unravel the cosmos, all gravity's spite.

## Signposts in the Cosmic Wilderness

In a forest of planets, where trees whistle tunes,
We search for the signs marked by silly raccoons.
With maps made of jelly and stars that all glow,
We navigate chaos like pros at a show.

Blasting off rockets of cream-filled delights,
Dancing with comets in zigzagging flights.
Through the fields of the odd, we make our own path,
Holding onto giggles like a mathematic's wrath.

## The Outcry of Silence

In the quiet, whispers roam,
Stars gossip in their cosmic home.
Galaxies spin with a cheeky grin,
While black holes chuckle, pulling us in.

The void shouts back with a silent shriek,
As photons play hide-and-seek.
Cosmic dust dances on a whim,
While time itself forgets to swim.

## Timeless Journeys and Celestial Questions

Space trains run on light-speed tracks,
Passengers rove in pajama slacks.
Where are we going? Oh, who knows!
Just watch out for the cosmic toes.

Wormholes bend, they twist and twine,
All aboard for a ride divine!
Questions float like socks in air,
Why is there cheese? Why is there hair?

## Navigating Through Celestial Skies

With a telescope, I take a peek,
At distant worlds that seem so bleak.
Comets come by with a cheerful wave,
Shooting stars misbehave, oh how they crave!

In this big sky, I ponder still,
Is that a planet, or breakfast grill?
Space cows moo from afar and tease,
While meteor showers rain down with ease.

## Wonders Beyond the Event Horizon

Beyond the haze where oddities dwell,
Something's calling, but who can tell?
A singing quasar, a dancing star,
They're just like us, minus the car!

With gravity playing such silly tricks,
We fall into space, just like the ticks.
Each moment spins with a wobbly grace,
In this vast dance of the cosmic race.

## Fractals of Existence

In every twist, a pattern shines,
We've got equations and coffee lines.
The cat in the hat is pondering wide,
While socks go missing, nowhere to hide.

Cosmic quarks do the mambo dance,
And rubber ducks join in the chance.
Galactic giggles echo through time,
As jellybeans orbit in silly rhyme.

Frogs on lily pads merge in a jig,
Turtles slide by, oh, what a big gig!
In this wondrous maze, we spin and twirl,
With a sprinkle of chaos, watch it unfurl.

Bubbles of joy float past our heads,
As unicorns visit in polka-dot threads.
Life's a circus, the tent's full of glee,
Let's juggle our worries, just you and me.

## Mosaic of Moments

We stitch together every joke,
With puns that make the cosmos smoke.
In a tapestry of awkward chat,
The stars giggle like a big, old cat.

Time's a pizza, sliced and diced,
With toppings of chaos, oh so spliced.
We dance through bits, quirky and bright,
As wormholes lead to a chocolate bite.

Squirrels debate the meaning of speed,
While rain clouds ponder a garden's need.
Each tick and tock's a funny sight,
As socks and sandals share the night.

Moments shimmer like disco balls,
As laughter echoes through cosmic halls.
With every giggle and snort they bring,
We crown the absurd, a lovely king.

## Radiant Realms and Mundane Journeys

In dusty corners, dust bunnies thrive,
While the toaster dreams of a five-star dive.
Dust motes waltz on a sunbeam's cheer,
As forks debate their pointy career.

Road trips filled with snacks and tunes,
While the GPS sings to the moons.
Frogs leap over philosophical streams,
As marshmallow clouds fulfill wild dreams.

Brushing off crumbs of outdated lore,
As chipmunks band together for more.
In this silly sketch of what we seek,
Naps are profound, and naps don't speak.

In every nook, the bright shines through,
While socks unite in a quirky crew.
So let's embrace this wondrous spree,
And laugh at the mundane, just you and me.

# Cosmic Choreography

The stars tango in a swirl of light,
While planets trip over cosmic height.
In a grand ballet with asteroids in tow,
They pirouette past the black hole's show.

Comets shimmy with eccentric flair,
As meteors manage a graceful air.
Through glittering trails of sparkling dust,
Even time and space have got to adjust.

Galaxies waltz in a swirling dress,
While moonbeams giggle, hardly a mess.
A disco ball in a nebula spins,
While gravitational pull tugs at our chins.

So join this dance that seems to defy,
With a twirl and a twist, let out a sigh.
For in this cosmic curious show,
We find the rhythm, and let laughter flow.

## Harmonies of Existence

In a cosmos where ducks wear hats,
And time is measured in furry cats,
Stars giggle, and planets dance,
While comets twirl in a silly prance.

The moon took a trip to learn ballet,
But tripped on a star and fell down to play.
Galaxies hum as they spin about,
Whispering secrets—without a doubt.

Jupiter's kitchen makes the best stew,
With sprinkles of stardust and potatoes, too.
Black holes sneak cookies when no one's around,
Grabbing the crumbs left behind on the ground.

So take a look up and see the show,
Where wonders roam free and laughter can grow.
In this grand jest that we call our fate,
Every twinkle and burst seems to celebrate.

## Eclipsed by Eternity

The sun wore shades during sunset bright,
As planets played cards, all in good light.
Time tried to tell a joke, but it slipped,
Now it's sat in the corner, its laughter zipped.

Saturn's rings are just hula hoops,
While black holes whisper to groups of goofs.
A star snorted stardust, what a sight,
And laughed with constellations all through the night.

Comets make wishes, they zoom and they swoosh,
But forget what to ask for in their dash and whoosh.
Eternity's got a funny knack,
For making each moment a cosmic snack.

So if you're feeling lost in the grand old play,
Just look for the jokes that the cosmos convey.
In this wacky realm where we giggle and spin,
There's always a punchline just waiting within.

## Journeys Through the Fabric of Time

Tick-tock said the clock, with a wink and a nod,
Trekking through moments, ain't it a prod?
The past wore pajamas, cozy and warm,
While the future wore shades, looking quite a charm.

Time-traveling llamas make grandiose trips,
Sipping on smoothies with fruity little sips.
They dance through the years, full of cheer,
Juggling the present while munching on beer.

In the timeline's threads, there's wayward yarn,
That unravels with tales that both giggle and warn.
Sometimes it hiccups, and then we all freeze,
While the clocks all conspire with pranks meant to tease.

So if you're clock-watching, why not take flight?
Join in the fun, let your worries take flight.
For in every tick, there's a laugh that's sublime,
We're all just the punchlines of journeying time.

## The Rift Between Dreams and Truth

In dreams, I see cats that can sing,
With tiny top hats, and a lovely bling.
But truth rolls its eyes and says, 'Not today,'
While spitting out sentences that just go grey.

Unicorns prance on the edge of the gray,
While socks fly off in a merry ballet.
The rift giggles softly, a whispery tease,
As dragons debate the best way to sneeze.

Reality peeks through a crack in the door,
Hoping to nap on a soft, fluffy floor.
But dreams are like children, they shout out loud,
Creating wild chaos, both happy and proud.

So let's raise a toast with imaginary cups,
To the rift that exists where imagination erupts.
For whether it's goofy or sounds quite absurd,
It's the harmony found that makes laughter heard.

### The Kaleidoscope of Possibilities

In a world of wobbly spins,
Colors clash with silly grins.
Everyone's a painter bright,
Drawing chaos day and night.

Hopping kangaroos, oh so grand,
With tap-dancing chairs that understand.
Curly fries in a marching band,
Twirling to a tune unplanned.

Clouds giggle in a puff of white,
While chairs compete in a leap of height.
Jelly beans swim in chocolate seas,
And rubber ducks ride the summer breeze.

So grab a hat, let's twirl around,
In this carousel of the upside-down.
With bubbles bursting into a cheer,
Life's a circus—come on, my dear!

## When Dreams Ignite the Cosmos

Stardust tickles sleeping cats,
As wishes bounce on sleepy mats.
Comets chase their own wild tails,
While marshmallow boats catch cosmic gales.

Coffee cups hold cosmic truths,
Winking at celestial sleuths.
Time travels on a pogo stick,
Making jokes both bold and quick.

Galaxies dance in polka dot flair,
With asteroids wearing stylish hair.
Giggles echo through the black,
As galaxies play a cosmic hack.

So dream a little dream tonight,
And join the stars in their silly flight.
On pixie dust, let's twirl and glide,
In this zany space where glee can't hide!

# The Compass of the Unknown

A compass spins with endless glee,
Pointing south to a tall, green tree.
It whispers secrets on the breeze,
Of hidden quirks and bumblebees.

Priorities lost in silly games,
As socks declare their own wild names.
Through labyrinths of giggles we roam,
Finding pizza is our true home.

Maps of jellybeans guide our way,
Through fields where the rubber chickens play.
With each turn, surprise awaits,
In a land where waltzing hedgehogs mate.

So let's embrace this crooked path,
With grins that spark spontaneous laugh.
Adventure breathes in the unknown,
Where even pencils feel at home!

## Shadows of Light and Dark

In shadow lanes where giggles creep,
The moonlight dances, never sleeps.
Puppies chase their bouncing tails,
While sunlight hums through winding trails.

Mashed potatoes in a silly stew,
Throwing shadows like they grew.
Light beams play tag with passing clouds,
Tickling laughter in cheerful crowds.

In the dark, a pickle winks,
And whispers how it surely shrinks.
Daydreams prank the sleepy night,
With bubblegum dreams that feel just right.

So stroll beneath the giggling stars,
Where shadows play their ukuleles and guitars.
In this mingling of light and shade,
The silly moments simply never fade!

## In the Shadow of Cosmic Giants

In a galaxy long passed, they say,
Stars danced wildly, bustled in play.
One star tripped over another's light,
Created a spark that lit up the night.

Nebulae giggled, swirling in the void,
Creating new worlds, some overjoyed.
Black holes snickered, their secrets unfurled,
Sucking in matter, lost in their world.

Comets dashed by with tails like kites,
Whispering jokes about silly delights.
Saturn showed off its rings with glee,
While Pluto pouted, "Hey, don't forget me!"

So amidst this cosmic circus we stand,
Striving for wisdom, with dreams in our hand.
With laughter and madness, we'll journey along,
In a realm of oddities where we all belong.

## Tales of Light and Darkness

In a realm where shadows play hide and seek,
A beam of sunshine began to speak.
"Oh, darkness! Why do you steal my shine?"
Darkness replied, "I just want to dine!"

A candle flickered, trying to brag,
But the moon said, "Stop, you're just a drag!"
Stars twinkled, chuckled, mocking the glare,
"We're the night's diamonds, beyond compare!"

A lone firefly buzzed, quite full of cheer,
"I'll outshine you all, just wait till I near!"
But it crashed into a porch, what a sight,
All the shadows roared with laughter that night.

Together they spun, a whimsical dance,
In this spectrum of chaos, a cosmic romance.
Between giggles and shimmers, they found their place,
In a universe where humor wears all the grace.

## Harbingers of Serendipity

Two planets collided, what a bizarre scene,
One yelled, "Oops! That was not in my routine!"
Asteroids laughed, lobbing little rocks,
While cosmic dust settled, mingling in flocks.

Whispers of comets around Uranus flew,
"Let's all throw a party, we'll call it a view!"
Gas giants bounced to a jovial tune,
Bouncing off clouds, beneath an odd moon.

A meteor jogged by, out of breath,
"I aimed for the stars, but missed to my death!"
While black holes chuckled, said, "Don't take it to heart,
You have all the time, let's make a new start!"

So let's raise a toast to bizarre cosmic fate,
To serendipity, spontaneity—great!
For amidst all the chaos, the laughter runs free,
In a tapestry woven of wild jubilee.

## The Alchemy of Breath and Stars

In a quiet corner, the cosmos sighed,
Stardust dribbled from the clouds wide.
With a sprinkle of laughter and a dash of delight,
The universe winked as it twinkled at night.

Galaxies swirled in a mischievous spree,
Making mud pies, as happy as can be.
A black hole grumbled, feeling rather blue,
"I want some fun too, what's wrong with you?"

Shooting stars dashed, hoping for wishes,
To tickle the planets and all of their fishes.
"What's your wish?" they winked, while flying in packs,
"To bake a cake without all the cracks!"

So spin your tales, let your laughter ignite,
For the alchemy of joy is a shimmering light.
In the canvas of space, filled with whimsy and cheer,
We find that the magic is always quite near.

# The Cosmic Dance of Existence

In a galaxy not too far,
Where planets play air guitar,
Stars giggle in swirling delight,
While comets race, zooming in flight.

Black holes take a break to yawns,
Nebulas bloom like cosmic fawns,
Asteroids argue about their style,
As aliens laugh in a cosmic smile.

## Whispers of Stardust and Shadows

In the shadows where stardust gleams,
Galactic squirrels plot their schemes,
A moonbeam sings a cheeky tune,
While robots dance beneath the moon.

Whispers float on cosmic air,
With jokes that only stars can share,
Galaxies chuckle, they can't resist,
Making all the black holes twist.

## Echoes of the Infinite

Echoes bounce from star to star,
Spreading giggles from afar,
Infinity wears a goofy grin,
As echoes echo back again.

Planets spin like playful tops,
While cosmic coffee never stops,
The universe hosts its wild show,
With punchlines only black holes know.

## Threads of Time and Space

Threads of time twist and tangle,
With silly knots that sometimes wrangle,
Time slips on banana peels,
While space folds like a giant wheel.

Twirling comets throw confetti,
In the chaos, things get petty,
But a giggle is what we choose,
As we glide in interstellar shoes.

## **Embracing the Chaos of Creation**

In a world where socks vanish,
And the dog thinks he can fly,
We chase after rhymes and laughter,
While the cats conspire nearby.

With every spill and joyful blunder,
We stumble through each grand design,
Chaos offers a dance in thunder,
As we sip on our cosmic wine.

So toss your plans like confetti,
Let the whims of fate unfurl,
In this circus of confetti,
Laughter is the greatest pearl.

Embrace the quirks, oh sweet errors,
For they color a dull routine,
In the mess, we find our heroes,
Where the silly chases the serene.

## The Art of Wandering in the Unknown

With a map upside down in hand,
I venture through bizarre terrains,
Accidental tourist, quite unplanned,
Collecting stories, losing chains.

Each step takes me to odd places,
Where the rules are just a joke,
Finding wisdom in silly faces,
With every stumble, a new poke.

From worlds where sandwiches dance,
To coffee that sings out loud,
I twirl in this whimsical chance,
In absurdity, I am proud.

So bring your quirks as you wander,
Let the journey twist and sway,
In the jest of life, we ponder,
Turning mundane into play.

## Eternal Echoes of Existence

In a void where nothing's certain,
I tripped over a cosmic star,
Got tangled in creation's curtain,
And laughed at how near I felt far.

Eons giggle in vast silence,
While I chase echoes of a rhyme,
Spinning tales like a mad science,
Crisp moments floating through time.

Galaxies waltz on a string,
As I drink tea with a black hole,
Whispers rise, as planets sing,
In the absurdity, I find my role.

So let's toast with a fizzy drink,
To the echoes that never cease,
In the chaos, let's pause and think,
We're all part of this cosmic piece.

# Fragments of a Cosmic Reverie

Stars sprinkle dreams like confetti,
Each wish a silly little jest,
In a realm that's oh so petty,
Where every second feels like a quest.

Oh look! A comet in pajamas,
Waving at the moon with glee,
Galactic jokes wrapped in dramas,
In spaces where we can't foresee.

Fragments of thoughts float around,
Tickled by the absurdity's glow,
In this kaleidoscope I've found,
The best stories come from the flow.

So take my hand, let's spin and twirl,
Through this wondrous cosmic spree,
In this party of stars, my girl,
Laughter's the answer, just let it be.

## Weaving the Fabric of Now

In a sock drawer, time is lost,
Each pair a memory, at what cost?
The cat pounces, takes a leap,
While we wonder, do socks dream deep?

Coffee spills, an artful mess,
Some say chaos, I call it finesse.
Juggling thoughts like rubber balls,
Hoping nothing breaks in the falls.

Buzzing phones serenade my ear,
A symphony of notifications near.
I respond 'yes', emojis in tow,
Wasn't that a meeting for a show?

Yet here in the now, we chuckle and glide,
Between bizarre moments, we find our stride.
The cosmic joke sat in plain view,
Twinkling with laughter, just like you.

## The Odyssey of Existence

A hamster wheel spins, a curious thing,
Is chasing my tail worthy of a king?
Every morning starts with a hopeful sigh,
At least today, I might touch the sky.

A sandwich talks back with each bite taken,
'You think you're quick—I'm bread, not shaken!'
The fridge hums softly, sharing its lore,
Of leftovers past that we can't ignore.

My socks have formed a mighty alliance,
They refuse to match; now that's defiance!
Meanwhile, dust bunnies dance in the light,
Plotting their reign, a fuzzy delight.

We tiptoe through time like a soft ballet,
Falling backward, then living today.
In this quirky quest, we all play our part,
With wisdom that's written upon a cart!

## Transcendence and the Unfathomable

In afternoons spent in a pondering gaze,
I count my years like broken displays.
What happens next? A deep, dark pit,
Is it wisdom gained or just sheer wit?

A sandwich philosopher, crumbs on my coat,
Ponder 'why not' as my thoughts stay afloat.
The coffee pot bubbles, pretends to be wise,
Whispering secrets as steam starts to rise.

Airplanes whisk by, in geometric arcs,
Do they know the sky hides marshmallow parks?
The planets align for a cosmic taco,
Galaxy spices—I'm ready! Oh, nacho!

We toast to the absurd—let's raise a cheer,
For mysteries wrapped in a riddle, my dear.
With giggles entwined in the fabric of fate,
We'll laugh and wait till it's all up to date.

## **Kaleidoscope of the Unknown**

Colors collide in a curious swirl,
I dropped my ice cream; watch it twirl!
As the sun sneezes and rainbows laugh,
We wonder aloud, 'What's the cosmic path?'

In spaceships made of cardboard and string,
We blast off to see what tomorrow might bring.
Elvis sings while pizza slices rhyme,
In a world where tales are woven with thyme.

The clock ticks backward; time's confused,
Jellyfish dance as humans are fused.
A dance-off ensues, the stars lose their shine,
While the moon rolls its eyes, 'Ain't this divine?'

So let's wear our mismatched socks with style,
Embrace the unknown and wear our best smile.
With dreams like balloons ready to soar,
We'll laugh at the wonders and ask for more!

## Requiem for the Forgotten Stars

In the night sky, they twinkle bright,
Dreams of cosmic pizza take flight.
Yet under their gaze, we stumble and trip,
Missing the message from their glowing blip.

Old stars whisper secrets of yore,
"Why so serious? We implore!"
Twirling in space with a cosmic joke,
They giggle from light-years as we choke.

Planets collide in a comical frame,
"Hey, is that Jupiter?" "No, it's just lame!"
A cosmic dance, with two left feet,
Gravitational pull, but can't find the beat.

Forgotten in dust, they flicker and fade,
Spaghetti scattered, a cosmic parade.
Raise a toast to the stars lost and free,
"They were here for a laugh, just like you and me!"

## Harmony in the Chaos of Being

In a blender of wishes, we swirl around,
Mixing our hopes in chaos profound.
With sprinkles of laughter and scoops of surprise,
We swirl and we twirl, oh how time flies!

Unicorns prance on rainbows so bright,
While penguins debate the meaning of flight.
A jester in galaxies, making us think,
"What's the point?" We chuckle and blink.

Balloons float high, while time does a jig,
Colors collide in a cosmic gig.
A playful design in this wobbly space,
Where chaos creates a quirky embrace.

So dance with the quarks, don't miss your chance,
Join in the jest of this wild cosmic dance!
In the chaos, we find rhythm with cheer,
And together we laugh as we sway without fear.

## The Serendipity of Cosmic Events

Stars plan a party, but forget the date,
Wormholes are late, and black holes just wait.
Meanwhile, comets crash in an awkward pose,
"Who invited that guy?" the universe knows.

Asteroids roll like clumsy stone balls,
Hitching a ride on gravity's calls.
Nearby, a nova throws confetti in style,
While supernovae dance, "Hey, stay for a while!"

With each little hiccup, the cosmos unfolds,
Tickling the fates with a giggle uncontrolled.
Serendipity laughing, oh what a sight,
As starlight slips by like a joke in the night.

So lift up your eyes and don't take a glance,
Join the ruckus, you might find romance.
In the dance of the stars, we stumble and sway,
Finding joy in the mishaps along the way.

# Galaxies in a Petri Dish

In a lab where the cosmos decides to play,
Galaxies swirl in a petri ballet.
With a sprinkle of stardust and a dash of glee,
They toss little quirks into our cosmic tea.

Microbe and quasar mix up a brew,
"Is that a new life form or just residue?"
With giggles of gravity, they tumble and spin,
Creating new worlds with a cheeky grin.

Bacteria dance as they wiggle about,
While dark matter grumbles, "What's this all about?"
The universe stirs in its microbial dish,
"More experiments, please, I'll grant you a wish!"

So grab your lab coat and plop down a seat,
Join the fun while the galaxies meet.
In this cosmic kitchen, don't be shy or aloof,
Laugh with the stars, that's the ultimate proof!

## Celestial Whispers and Silent Spheres

Stars gossip in the night,
As the moon rolls its eyes,
Galaxies crack a joke,
And black holes chuckle in disguise.

Planets play hide and seek,
While comets try to race,
Meteors swear it's not their fault,
For falling from their place.

Nebulas puff up their chests,
Claiming beauty is their game,
While asteroids munch on space rocks,
And twinkle with no shame.

It's a cosmic joke for all,
A circus up above,
Where even the sun beams brightly,
Laughing with a shove.

## The Dance of Time and Stardust

Tick-tock goes the cosmic clock,
As stardust swirls about,
Time waltzes with a comet's tail,
While galaxies jump and shout.

Seconds spin like twirling stars,
In a ballroom made of blue,
Where every tick's a chance to laugh,
And every tock's a 'who knew?'.

Wormholes twist and twine with glee,
Invisible to the eye,
Yet ticklish to the touch, you see,
As they giggle passing by.

Dancing shadows chase their tails,
In constellations we can't trace,
While time itself just smirks and smiles,
In this never-ending space.

## Threads of Fate in the Cosmic Loom

Weaving stars with silver threads,
The cosmos hums a tune,
While fate stitches up the night,
Underneath the chuckling moon.

Black holes gulp and belch out light,
Dancing in their gravity,
While meteors glide through fabric,
As smooth as they can be.

Galactic yarn spun tight with jokes,
Knitting dreams into the dark,
Each thread a story waiting,
To leave its silly mark.

Spools of time roll with abandon,
As comets laugh and glide,
In this fabric of existence,
Where whimsy takes a ride.

## Infinity's Embrace

In the arms of endless wonder,
Sighing stars stretch wide,
As humorous echoes of the past,
Greet us with a chuckled pride.

Eternity winks with mischief,
As atoms dance in glee,
While galaxies mix up their names,
In this adorable spree.

Dimensions twirl in silly shapes,
Tickling our perception,
And mysteries wrapped in giggles,
Fill the void with affection.

Oh, how time flips and flops,
In this endless cosmic race,
With laughter echoing for ages,
In infinity's warm embrace.

## Stardust Stories

In a galaxy not so far,
Little aliens play guitar.
They sing to comets passing by,
While sipping tea and eating pie.

Stars chuckle at their silly tunes,
Dancing 'neath the silver moons.
UFOs in a conga line,
Trip on their own spaghetti vine.

When black holes start to swallow light,
They pull out glow sticks for a fight.
With disco balls that spin so fast,
They party like there's no vast past.

So if you ever hear a tune,
From distant worlds beneath the moon,
Just know it's not your average jam,
But stardust singing—yes, it's glam!

## Shadows of Yesterday

Every shadow that we cast,
Has stories from the distant past.
A sock that disappeared one day,
Might just be on a holiday.

Ghosts of socks in limbo roam,
Wishing they could just go home.
Waltzing in corners, having fun,
While lint bunnies bask in the sun.

Time travelers in a time loop,
Count sheep that jump, then form a troop.
They blend with curtains, snooze away,
Inventing fandoms of their day.

So if you glimpse a shadow play,
Know it's yesterday's grand ballet.
It's probably just shadows of fun,
Dancing until the morning sun.

## Light of Tomorrow

Chasing beams of bright delight,
Tomorrow's glow is in our sight.
With neon shades and funky hats,
We zoom around like hyper cats.

In a race to catch the dawn,
With vintage bikes and unicorns.
We zip through clouds of cotton candy,
While singing songs that get quite randy.

Tomorrow's light is quite a tease,
It tickles noses, brings us ease.
But catch it quick, it might just hide,
Behind a comet's sweeping stride.

So let's not fret or count the hours,
Instead, let's dance amongst the flowers.
For the light ahead is all a jest,
The best of jokes is what we quest!

## The Heartbeat of an Infinite Sky

The sky laughs with a playful grin,
Pulsating stars where dreams begin.
Clouds trade secrets, giggle and sway,
While sunbeams peek in a cheeky way.

A heartbeat felt in cosmic rays,
Tickles comets in a dance of hoorays.
Planets spin with mischievous flair,
Whispering jokes from atmosphere air.

Saturn's rings have hugs to share,
As shooting stars make wishes rare.
Cosmic laughter, oh what a treat,
In the vastness where wonders meet.

So if you find a star that winks,
Just know it's time to share some drinks.
For in this heartbeat of the sky,
The funny tales of space fly high!

## Cosmic Waves and Winding Roads

On cosmic waves, we ride for fun,
Chasing stardust, making the run.
These winding roads of asteroid dust,
Map out journeys filled with trust.

Each twist and turn, a silly trip,
With space donuts for a snack, take a sip.
Comets zooming, zany and fast,
Panicking pilots—not meant to last!

Aliens salute with goofy grins,
While galaxies spin in dizzying spins.
Navigating laughter in the void,
Finding joy, never feeling paranoid.

So if you steer through cosmic fun,
Remember to laugh—you're not done.
With every wave and road ahead,
Silly stories will be bred!

## Wanderers Amongst the Celestial Bodies

We drift through space like lost socks,
Chasing stars and cosmic knocks.
Comets tailing, oh what a sight,
Mismatched wonders dancing at night.

Aliens laugh at our silly quirks,
While we ponder, engrossed in our perks.
With ice cream in hand, we float and glide,
In this grand cosmic goofy ride.

Asteroids wink as they pass us by,
Whispering secrets from the sky.
Planetary parties, a jovial scene,
Amidst endless laughter, a shared routine.

Gravity's a prankster, it pulls us down,
While we dream of capers in a starry gown.
What a ballet of quips and glee,
In this vast playground of mystery.

## The Symphony of Silent Worlds

In realms where silence takes its stand,
The music's played by an unseen hand.
Yet here we are, in cosmic jest,
Humming tunes that never rest.

Planets spin in a wobbly tune,
Mars argues with a sarcastic moon.
Jupiter's got the bass on lock,
As melodies bounce like a friendly rock.

Comets whistle with a cheeky flair,
While black holes play hide and seek with air.
Oh, what a ruckus among the stars,
As cosmic pranksters wave from afar.

Bouncing rhythms beyond our reach,
Stars giggle, no lessons to teach.
In this odd, hitchhiker's kind of jam,
The grand symphony plays, "Who gives a damn?"

## Between Dreams and Reality

Caught in a bind of what's a dream,
Thoughts parade in a silly stream.
Between the stars, I toss and turn,
For wisdom burned, I yearn and yearn.

Do I sleepwalk through the cosmic fair?
With cosmic giggles floating in the air.
Each distracted thought leads me astray,
Like a lost sock on laundry day.

Glimpses of grandeur become mere fables,
As I mix my dreams with old Robin's tables.
The lines are blurred, reality's a tease,
As I dance with shadows and the cosmic breeze.

Unrehearsed, our stories unfold,
While giggling galaxies we behold.
In this intertwine, we make a laugh,
Crafting narratives from each quirky half.

## Stardust Dreams and Celestial Schemes

With stardust dreams in our pockets tight,
We jump through portals of pure delight.
Scheming with stars, cheeky as can be,
Creating worlds with a cosmic spree.

In the kitchen of space, we bake a cake,
In layers of planets, for goodness' sake.
Add sprinkles of comets, a frosting swirl,
Who knew a kitchen could dance and twirl?

Every neutron dances a playful jig,
As we plot the universe's next big big.
A pinch of chaos, a dash of fun,
Mixing up creation, here we run!

With laughter echoing through the void,
Outrageous dreams we've all enjoyed.
Stardust laughs echo loud and clear,
As we toast to the stars with cosmic cheer.

## Dissonance and Harmony of Existence

In a dance of quirks and fate,
Juggling fruit on a dinner plate,
Socks on hands, shoes on cats,
We laugh at the oddities, imagine that!

Mismatched socks in a laundry maze,
A fish that sings in a glittery daze,
Balloons that argue about who's the best,
As we ponder these puzzles, it's all a jest!

The toaster sings while the kettle hums,
A clock that ticks in reverse drums,
Bees that rhyme while sipping tea,
Oh, how absurd this world can be!

Yet in the chaos, joy it brings,
Like dancing with owls and flapping wings,
In disarray, we find our song,
Embracing the weirdness, where we belong!

## Patterns in the Ether

Stars align like spaghetti strands,
At a picnic on faraway lands,
Aliens play hopscotch on Mars,
While squirrels debate the shape of stars.

Clouds passing gossip, whispering light,
As shadows tango, what a sight!
Raindrops are tap dancers on the street,
As the sun takes a bow, this show's a treat!

Chasing shadows with a giggle and cheer,
The moon's wearing pajamas, oh dear!
Patterns emerge from the whimsical haze,
Where laughter bursts forth in endless displays.

Let's sketch the chaos in bright crayon hues,
And paint the nonsense with silly views,
For what's a dance with no funny prance?
In the ether we twirl, given a chance!

## The Labyrinth of Creation

In the maze of thoughts, a rabbit hops,
Wearing a hat with polka dot flops,
Winding through corridors of whimsical thought,
Playing hide and seek, oh what a plot!

A pudding cat sings operatic tunes,
While carrots wear hats and sleep with spoons,
Mirrors reflect the silly and sweet,
As imagination gets up on its feet!

Giraffes ride bicycles, oh what a sight,
Under lampshades glowing, so bright,
The walls are made of jelly and dreams,
In this wild place where nonsense redeems.

Let's wander these paths, hand in hand,
Following the laughter, so unplanned,
In the labyrinth where whims collide,
Creation takes a joyful ride!

## Where Time Does Not Tread

In a realm where clocks forget their ticks,
And rabbits juggle balancing tricks,
The sun wears a party hat of joy,
Welcoming wonders, a child's toy.

Trees hold secrets in their bark,
While shadows play cards after dark,
Whimsical whispers from the breeze,
A serenade that aims to please.

Marshmallow clouds float up so high,
While worries wander and say goodbye,
In the absence of clocks, we get to roam,
In a timeless land that feels like home.

So join the frolic in moments that cheer,
With laughter ringing out loud and clear,
In this space where moments can bend,
We find our joy, with no end!

## Where Galaxies Converge

Stars collide with a clumsy cheer,
Dancing in space, oh dear, oh dear!
Black holes giggle as they spin,
While comets race, not sure who'll win.

Nebulas pop like confetti streams,
Planets stumble, bursting dreams.
Shooting stars need a map to flee,
Who knew they'd be so hard to see?

Aliens wink from their silver ships,
Telling jokes with wobbly quips.
Asteroids throw a cosmic party,
But bumping into them? Quite dirty!

In this vast cosmic mess we grin,
Where space is fun and the chaos begins.
So sip your stardust, take a spin,
And dance with the galaxies, let's dive in!

## The Pulse of Time's Embrace

Tick-tock giggles through the ages,
Time wears silly, colorful pages.
Yesterday wore an outfit bright,
While tomorrow juggles with delight.

Yesterday's leftovers are stale and cold,
But time's a tease, always bold.
It plays hide and seek with each new day,
And tickles our noses, making us sway.

Moments slip, like slippery fish,
Wishing for a cosmic swish.
Yet here we are, just keeping track,
Buddy, please, don't fall off the rack!

So laugh with the seconds, make them dance,
Twirl with the hours, give time a chance.
For every minute has a funny tease,
In this wild ride, let's giggle with ease!

## A Voyage Through Cosmic Seas

Surfing waves of stardust bright,
Bumping into comets—what a sight!
Galactic tide pulls us away,
Splashing through moons, come what may.

Asteroids sing in spooky tunes,
While spaceship sails chase glowing moons.
Constellations play a game of chess,
What a galactic, wondrous mess!

Black holes whirl like cosmic sinks,
Swallowing thoughts, and quite a few drinks.
Planets try to catch the waves,
Aboard our ship, all misbehavior braves!

So ride the currents, lose your shoe,
In this ocean of stars, it's all brand new.
With laughter echoing through the breeze,
Join this voyage with playful ease!

## Reflections in the Void

In the void, where nothing's found,
Mirrors giggle without a sound.
Shadows play peek-a-boo with light,
As the cosmos paints the night so bright.

Echoes of jokes swirl in the air,
When you're alone, but you don't care.
Void whispers secrets that make you grin,
"Next cosmic wave, let the fun begin!"

Sparkles wink from the empty space,
Playing tag in an endless race.
Reflections laugh at the silent stare,
In the nothingness, we bounce with flair.

So if you find yourself out there,
Don't fret, the void's a cheeky affair.
Join the echoes, let laughter thrive,
In the emptiness, we feel alive!

## Reflections in the Mirror of Galaxies

In a cosmic shop, I bought a smile,
They said it's good for travel a while.
But every time I grin so wide,
The stars just laugh, they can't decide.

With planets spinning, hats askew,
Whirling thoughts in cosmic glue.
Asteroids roll past with a shout,
"Hey, buddy! What's this fuss about?"

My mirror's cracked, but that's okay,
It shows me colors bright and gay.
I wave to comets, they wave back,
Each one a spark in the endless black.

Gazing deep into the void,
Jokes emerge, oh so overjoyed.
Reflecting back from stars that twinkle,
I'm just a speck, with a nervous wrinkle.

## Chasing Shadows of Distant Suns

I sprint to catch a beam of light,
Only to trip—oh, what a sight!
The sun just chuckles, warms the chill,
While I'm tangled in a cosmic thrill.

Outrunning shadows, it's such a race,
But beams of laughter fill the space.
I asked a star for some wise advice,
It winked and said, "Just be nice!"

Planets bloom, they're sprightly fair,
While I'm still tangled in mid-air.
Like jellybeans in a cosmic swirl,
My thoughts bounce 'round in a starry whirl.

So I chase my dreams, and they slip away,
But the light brings joy, come what may.
With every step, I'll find my fun,
In shadows dancing by distant suns.

## The Poetry of the Infinite Journey

In a spaceship made of candy bars,
I traveled far, beyond the stars.
Eating stardust, sipping on air,
My diet's strange, but I don't care.

I penned a poem on a comet's tail,
It's quite a ride; I can't derail.
The ink may smudge, the rhymes may slip,
But who needs rules on this wild trip?

Galactic highways twist and spin,
Where space-time's elastic and quirks begin.
I asked a black hole, "What's the goal?"
It grinned and said, "To take a stroll!"

So here I float, on whims I soar,
With laughter echoing, forever more.
My poetry weaves through the stars like beams,
Creating laughter amidst cosmic dreams.

## When Stars Collide: A Love Story

Two stars met in a drunken spin,
Twirled around till they fell in.
"Do you believe in fate?" one said,
The other laughed, "Just go to bed!"

They crashed with flair, a cosmic spark,
Danced away, leaving a mark.
With quirks and giggles, their orbits entwined,
Love in the cosmos, so well-defined.

Nebulas cheered, meteor showers cried,
While comets twirled in a joyful glide.
A love so bright, with fireworks wide,
The universe sighed, they'd never hide.

So here's to the stars, who boldly collide,
Creating laughter with every ride.
In the vastness of space, love takes flight,
Making the cosmos a little more bright.

## Wandering the Hiatus of Space

In a vacuum where snacks disappear,
I float with my chips, just a bit of fear.
Gravity's off, but my cravings persist,
With a bag of popcorn, I simply can't resist.

Stars twinkle like disco balls at night,
But my compass is broken, I can't take flight.
Navigating through cosmic carousels,
Every spin leaves me with dizzy spells.

I call up the sun for some midday cheer,
But it laughs and says, 'I'm too hot; disappear!'
Comets zoom past with their wild, bright tails,
And I try to catch one, but I'm destined to fail.

So I tinker with rockets made from soda straws,
Building my dreams while defying all laws.
In this grand show of the stellar soap opera,
I'm the clueless star, and the audience is "Who's here?"

## The Intermission of Existence

Between every laugh, there's a sigh,
As interludes linger, and double the pie.
Time's on a break, sipping tea with fate,
Even clocks go slow, it's a perfect date.

I asked a tree about wisdom to glean,
It said, 'Branch out!' with a wink and a green.
The rocks have opinions; they sit and they gawk,
While ants hold a conference, debating the walk.

My shoes are all mismatched; I call it my style,
When I trip over stardust, I take it with guile.
A flickering star tossed me a wink,
And I giggled, forgetting how to think.

Though every pause has its odd little quirks,
I count my odd socks, and the universe smirks.
I burst into laughter, at cosmic delays,
As I order some fries from the Milky Way's bays.

# Threads of Stardust Fables

Once an asteroid danced on a whim,
It tripped on a comet, its chances were slim.
The cosmos held stories, bizarre and absurd,
With planets who whispered like birds unheard.

A black hole's a vacuum, or so they presume,
While aliens giggle, plotting comic gloom.
I tossed them a riddle; they returned with a joke,
Now space is a comedy club, what a stroke!

Nebulas knit warmth from threads of pure light,
Making sweaters for stars on the coldest of nights.
Galaxies spiral, they dance in a line,
Each twirl sending ripples through the fabric of time.

So here in this galaxy, quirky and bright,
We stitch up the fables and shine through the night.
A laugh and a wink, what more could we need?
As we sip on our stardust and plan our next deed.

## Uncharted Destinies

With a map made of giggles, I chart my own course,
In a spaceship of paper, I harness my force.
Bumping into meteors, oh what a sight,
One winked back and asked if I wanted a bite.

Planets play hopscotch, the asteroids cheer,
As I float by, doing the cosmic rear.
I tried a cartwheel, but spun out of bounds,
And landed in laughter, in jovial sounds.

The space-time continuum threw a surprise,
Inviting me backward to see how I rise.
With a tickle and giggle from the fabric of fate,
I found that each stumble was more than just great.

With every odd twist and each playful loop,
I gather my friends in this stellar troupe.
Together we wander, through giggles and dreams,
Uncharted, but happy, or so it all seems.

## Echoes of the Unseen

In the shadows, things do prance,
Chasing dreams, we take a chance,
Stars are laughing from afar,
Or maybe that's just my car.

Planets spinning, quite the show,
Who knew they had such flair to glow?
Aliens sipping cosmic tea,
Saying, "Earthlings, let it be!"

## Embracing the Unknown

I stumbled 'pon a cosmic clue,
The cat's out, but where's the shoe?
With each step, I trip and sway,
Chasing mysteries every day.

Curiosity's a funny beast,
Leaves me hungry, never ceased,
I asked a comet, 'Tell me more!'
It winked and zipped right past the door.

## Galactic Tales Unfolding

A black hole shared a joke with me,
Said, 'I suck at parties, can't you see?'
Asteroids chuckled, rolling 'round,
While shooting stars just stood their ground.

The sun's too bright, it's got a glare,
Hiding secrets in its fiery hair,
The moon just giggles, shy and white,
Hoping we won't stare too trite.

## Whispers of the Celestial Clock

Tick-tock goes the cosmic dream,
With dashing lights, it takes the beam,
Rabbits sprint through space and time,
Their tales are silly, small, and prime.

Galaxies winking, stars so bright,
Dancing through the starry night,
Count your socks, don't lose your keys,
Even space gets its own quirks, you see?

## Whirlwinds of Chance and Choice

In the dance of fate, we spin,
Twirling in our silly skin.
Waffles or pancakes, what a plight,
Choosing wrong could start a fight.

A sock's retreat, it dares to flee,
Hiding from its mate, you see.
Flip a coin, heads or tails?
One way, you buy, the other fails.

In a world of chance, we skip,
Like jellybeans on a road trip.
Pick a color, red or blue,
Trust your gut—it's up to you.

When recipes go off the track,
Pasta's pudding? Better crack!
Sometimes it's chaos, pure delight,
In this whirlwind, hold on tight.

## Reverberations of the Cosmic Heart

Stars giggle as they twinkle bright,
Sending whispers through the night.
Gravity's pull, a cosmic prank,
Caught in orbit, we're all a quank.

Aliens laugh on distant shores,
Wondering if we'll ever score.
With odd-shaped fruit and flying cars,
We ponder deeply, 'Who are we, stars?'

The sun's a joker, shining bold,
Warming up our tales untold.
Clouds float high; they start to tease,
Rain or shine, we'll take it with ease.

In this grand cosmic ballet dance,
We twirl with fate, give it a chance.
Laughter echoes off the moon,
Cosmic heart plays a funny tune.

## The Overlap of Dreams and Reality

One minute you're soaring through space,
Next, at the market, you lose your place.
Chasing a dream in your jammies late,
Oops! Now you're late for a dinner date!

Your cat is a tiger, fierce and wild,
Yet on your lap, it's just a child.
Reality bends and so does your spoon,
Eating soup in the afternoon.

Open your eyes, the mirror grins,
Is it you, or where have you been?
Pillow fights turn to cosmic showdowns,
Break out the starship, let's wear our crowns!

With daydreams swirling in the breeze,
We navigate through life with ease.
Between the worlds we love to play,
In this silly dance, we'll find our way.

## Celestial Echoes of Our Stories

We weave our tales with stardust threads,
Laughing at the paths we've fled.
Comets race to spread the news,
Who knew our fumbles would amuse?

In the tale of a wayward shoe,
Could it be magic? Who knew?
Stars align in a quirky spin,
Finding our treasures where we've been.

Galaxies swirl with gossip in tow,
As moonbeams giggle, softly aglow.
Strange curiosities spark the night,
Funny fables take wing in flight.

Let's raise a toast to all we share,
A universe ripe with joy and flair.
Through echoes bright, our stories sing,
In this cosmic circus, we're all on a swing!

## Curiosities of the Cosmic Tapestry

Stars play poker, moon's a dealer,
Comets crash, and Venus squeals.
Galaxies spin like cotton candy,
While black holes laugh at how we feel.

Zebras roam on Saturn's rings,
Dancing with the Martian kings.
Jupiter's a giant named Lou,
Who tells the best jokes, don't you think, too?

Asteroids quack in wobbly flight,
As nebulas glimmer with delight.
Every supernova's just a sneeze,
In this cosmic circus, if you please.

So grab your hat and join the show,
With prancing stars, in bubbly glow.
The cosmic swirl is wild and free,
A delight for all, just wait and see!

## Celestial Navigators

Captain Quasar steers with flair,
His trusty crew, a bunch of bears.
They chart their course through candy cane,
While shooting stars sing in the rain.

Pulsars twinkle like disco balls,
Inviting aliens to moonlit calls.
They bring their drinks in fizzy cups,
And toast to planets, upside-down ups.

Uranus chuckles at the jest,
"Who knew I'd be the cosmic best?"
Rosy Martians dance in their suits,
Cracking jokes in their furry boots.

So join the crew, just grab a snack,
As meteors line up for a snack attack.
With laughter echoing through the void,
In this starry fun, we're all employed!

## Where Echoes Meet the Horizon

Echoes sing on cosmic breeze,
Whispers shared beneath the trees.
Saturn's rings are big and bright,
Filtering echoes into the night.

Galactic giggles bounce around,
While superclusters make silly sounds.
Neptune joins in on the fun,
Making waves that weigh a ton.

The horizon plays peekaboo,
With bright ideas and a zesty hue.
Every shout's a festive call,
Drawn in stardust, we share it all.

Let's laugh with lightning in the sky,
And wave at meteors speeding by.
For in this dance among the sighs,
We find our joy where echoes rise!

## Flux and Form

Shapes in space, they wiggle-wobble,
Asteroids play, but never dawdle.
Nebulae puff like cotton fluff,
Creating art that's quite enough.

Time spins in circles, what a whirl!
While comets chase a dancing girl.
With humor packed in every beam,
They bend and twist, as if in a dream.

Galaxies snicker, "What's the plan?"
"We'll just take selfies—'cause we can!"
In this show of cosmic sport,
Every crack-up is a court.

So let's embrace the whimsy here,
As starlight tickles, brings us cheer.
In a flux of form that always bounces,
We ride the tide where laughter flounces!